THAT INFINITE ROAR

by
Laurie Kuntz

Gyroscope Press

Gyroscope Press
PO Box 1989
Gillette, WY 82717
gyroscopepress@gmail.com

That Infinite Roar

ISBN: 978-1-7367820-5-7
Published in the United States of America

Dedication:
Roar On: Noah and Lau

Table of Contents

That Infinite Roar

"A whisper can become a roar"

—Gena Showalter

I Need a Title

for a new collection
of recent poems.
My top choice:
"First Snow, Last Rose,"
you frowned, *not again with flowers,*
stay away from roses and moons and Junes,
My second choice:
"The Empty Heart,"
No hearts, no pinks, no puff of clouds. . .
All that I hoped for, you rejected.
I begged a title to yell that infinite roar
I hear in my heart, that I see in every pink
bud of the first rose that I wait for,
or in the moon waxing its round voice.
Then, there is that first snow
that bides me to hibernate, then renew.
What about that infinite roar?

ANNIVERSARY, AGAIN

I don't know a love that does not chip away
at the day to day of what couples us.
Every act of creation, also an act of destruction,
and memory is history's great reviser.

The years pass, the regrets mount,
but so does the shared light
we both enjoy at sunset.
And, there's the song of the brown thrasher
hidden in our magnolia tree.

We strain to catch a glimpse before it flies—
this memory implanted on its wingspread
soaring away with a piece of what's been shared.

Things we mark as love
belong in no engraved setting,
but in the dusting of grey hairs off the vanity,
the sweeping of the dead
palmetto bug from under the porch light,
ripe pears in a bowl placed on a table,
all marking the tart juice of our shared years.

The days pass as starlings ignore
the boundaries of the skyway.
We remain together under the weight
of every season, standing some days
on a stark precipice weaving stories
into our own private landscape,
all we let in under the presence

of every necessary ripening thing
like these collected years.

OLD MARRIED COUPLE CUTTING WATERMELON

There are some things
we just don't do well together.
I am not your tennis partner.
There are some mountains you climb alone.
I cannot sing while you tune your guitar.
But, we have learned the rhythm of
a couple with a cleaver.

We both know how to check for ripeness.
A lawn green skin with a yellow sun
bursting at its center.
An ear to the rind,
checking for the sea caught in a shell sound.

At home, we prepare the counter,
find a balance so the orb does not roll,
fill containers with ruby red squares
that will quench our aging thirst.

One July day, while you napped
the temperature grew thick
as watermelon skin.
Alone in the kitchen, I tackled the green ball
with a serrated edge,
found the sweet spot on the counter
to conquer the roll, sliced the fruit
in halves and quarters until plates were glowing
with squares looking like polished gems.

What I thought was a job for two,
I could do by myself—
handle a knife, square a slice, dispose of rinds,
fill a bowl that only I would gorge from,
a selfish appetite quenched.

Alone, in the kitchen
I picked the ripest pieces,
but the juices did not burst,
nor run over my tongue
with the same coupled sweetness.

KOMOREBI

Walking the dogs uphill
in a borrowed country on borrowed time
concentrating on my old steps
you, still on level ground, call me back
to look at the light through the trees
komorebi, you pronounce it slowly
then remind me the needed translation
as we continue on the steep gravel path,
our lights, like the splintered rays
through the high pines are dimming daily,
but we still attempt these sheer walks
breathing heavily together.

MAKING PEACE WITH A DEAD PALMETTO BUG IN THE TIME OF COVID

You, my bug whisperer,
warding scorpions off walls,
and cornering huge Palmetto bugs
that inch into the shower.
I rely on you with that sure
and steady swat of flip flop in hand.

Then, in time for rainy season,
when all the winged and armored critters
not so unlike us, seek refuge
inside stalls and cornered crevices,
you got COVID.

I could not sink to a low point
to ask you in your feverish state
to pick up the already gone Palmetto
from the shower drain.

So, dust pan and broom in hand,
open toilet bowl, clenched teeth, white knuckles
I scooped and flushed, making peace
with small inconveniences, while waiting
for you in grace of strength and favors
to feel more like yourself,
and regain that sure and steady swat.

NORTH OF SORROW

What can save us from turning
life into an ash of regret?
Words no longer work to meaning
and the ear tunes to a screech, pitch, and wail.
Every sound byte, one that reminds us
not of the whisper of breeze
billowing sheets drying in the sun,
but the entrapment of the twist
and entanglement of those same sheets
wet and caught in a wringing wind.
Everyone waits for hope
to blow through an open window,
for all that is on the outside
can enter a home, a heart, a memory,
and north of sorrow
are the lit borders,
which we can cross.

THE POEM YOU WILL NEVER READ

It was our ritual:
A birthday poem for a new
rotation around our fading suns.

A Libra birthday, for balance,
but our balance is outweighed
by a wall of anger.

Sometimes, I see a movie
about a woman and her cat,
read a Rexroth poem,
sip a cup of chamomile tea,
and think to reach out,

but I can't, even on this day,
a day I often pen with words for you.

I'm still drawn to the Muse in the ashes
as old as the ancient stone gargoyle
hanging on the awning of my house,
which you no longer enter.

Old habits, like love, hard to break.

BALANCE

The girl on the dirt road rides a thick tire bike
with ease, skimming over sun streaked rocks
that match the bows in her braided hair,
the streamers whisper at upturned handlebars,
and her red laces flap against white trimmed
pedals.

Not so long ago someone taught her,
held the back seat while running alongside,
spoke of stability and rhythm
in a voice that conquered all fears.

That sturdy weight of trust cradled
in one hand buoyed all to balance
when it lifted like a feathered wing
off the shore and let her glide
into the only life she would ever know to choose.

"I have my way of praying, as you no doubt have yours."

Mary Oliver

PRAYER

A poet once said "I have my way of praying. . . "
Isn't a poem just a prayer
the call for a beginning and end,
words we dress in figurative evening wear,
with a top hat for a title.

We all have our ways to follow,
to treasure the little that can save us,
whether it be birdsong
heard through a frosted window,
light that settles on the sill,
or the red road dust that sings
from our swirling skirts.

THERE ARE NO WORDS

on the murder of Tyre Nichols

There are no words,
yet many a word, but they are buried
with hope for any kind of humanity,
which has left the building along with
those garnering wishes to be in places
on a variegated map in which all routes
lead to those lost—
lost in madness, apathy, injustice,
in the cry for a loving mother,
and a loving mother's cry
for the rest of humanity,
which can speak in kind whispers,
lead us home to a simple verbal hug—
Yeah, those words.

A HOWL IN THE WIND: A RESPONSE TO THE OVERTURNING OF ROE V. WADE

How terribly strange to be impregnated
by an uncle, a father, a neighbor,
a teacher, a doctor.
Remaining silent at 17,
carrying the attack,
untold for fear.

You are at fault.
You are to blame.
You are wrong.

You are less than your father,
your neighbor, your teacher, your doctor.

How terribly strange to know
you have no voice, but to remain silent—
silent at 18, at 33, at 41.
You feel less
than all the power men amass.

How terribly strange to have a dark secret,
but somewhere in the telling
these voices can resound and carry
a howl in the wind to resist, yet again.
You live, she lives, we live to choose,
Me two, Me three, Me many,
we cannot, will not, be silenced to the grave.

WHAT MY SISTERS SHOULD KNOW BEFORE I DIE

I never envied you
but stood in ovation,
swallowed your essence
as if an elixir.

I felt a comfort
walking beside you
on red dirt trails,

naming tropical flowers
exotic names, luring
us to our own selves.

I reveled in your secrets,
kept them under my tongue
like a lingering slice of guava.

I never judged
even when you held back on the truth,
which saves us when shared.

For it is in the sharing
from our clasped hands
that our true wings sprout.

WHAT THE DEAD CAN USE

My sister wanted to slip
the gold ring with diamond chips
back on my dead mother's finger,
or was it her pearl necklace,
or charm bracelet?

What I remember
is it was shiny, something of value.

The rabbi on guard at my mother's coffin,
admonished my sister
who was about to dress
the dead with jewels.

Doing his job, the rabbi
advised my sister to keep
the ring as an heirloom
having no worth to those in a coffin.

But when the mourners turned their backs,
my grief-stricken sister slipped
the ring onto our mother's ghostly finger.

Seven years gone,
I imagine mother's bones
dried and crumbled to dust,
but still on her brittle ring finger,
a gold band strewn
with diamonds shines,
still of use.

MY MOTHER'S WEDDING RING

was very different
not the traditional gold band
but a swerve of rubies around
an 18-karat indent of ore.

I loved that ring,
but not the marriage it circled,
felt for my mother and her burden
of a weakened commitment.

But, I loved the thick band of clouded sunset metal.

I am now as old as she was when she handed me
the ring, saying that I should wear it
while she was alive so she could see my joy,
but that day, fearful of wear,
I put it away for safekeeping.

What is safe these days?
Not a marriage, nor a child,
hardly a country, or its people.

So, today, in the midst of
"Nothing gold can stay"
I take my mother's wedding ring
out of safekeeping,
put it on my finger,
and let those rubies glisten.

THE FREEDOM FROM BEING BEAUTIFUL
> after a line in the poem *"Menopause"*
> by C. Prudence Arceneaux

All that work:

The manicured body,
replenished skin,
and the avoidance of the syrupy desires,
the lusting glow of everything bronze.

Hair managed, eyes shadowed,
the arched and high cheekbone turning
into the right angle, away from the sun,
and anything else that might burn through the
work.

The nightly rituals, the glossy cover photo
touched up, but never touched, never knowing
the comfort of what can be discovered
in the uncovering of one's uncharted skin.

My Wisteria

Stagnant in December, a bare stick clinging
to a trellis—like a woman
stranded in the wind without the proper overcoat.

Memories of cicada filled nights,
and perfume, its scent
misting veranda lamps with ribbons of light
pouring on purple petals.

She remembers:

A lilac shawl draped over her.
In her season,
she was cloaked in everything that flowered.

Now, another year etches
itself on her gnarled branches.

She has no choice but to be content
until the murmurs
Of all that blooms purple

happen, yet once again.

"...the world offers itself to your imagination, calls to you like the wild geese, harsh and exciting—"

Mary Oliver

First Banana

When all waxing ounces
of your premature weight
reached 5 pounds, you were allowed
first solids—we fed you a banana,
and you growled like an animal in waiting.
The mushy pulp around your feathered mouth,
muscles barely ready to chew
swallowed the mashed fruity slime.
After tubes of formula, pumped breast milk,
and colicky evenings,
you swallowed a sweetness,
that there were no words for, just a growl,
that first joy, that infinite roar.

TWIGS AND TRINKETS

When you were a child,
every remnant of a stick,
a lost button, a flattened penny,
that random feather in the grass
was a gift from the *fairy godmother*,
who knew our every step, our planned journeys
to the market, movie, or park.
Ball and bat in hand, this was magic,
not the disappearing kind, but the magic
of what can be rescued from under a tree,
in a sidewalk crack, or from a trinket
left on a wooden park bench.
Random gifts, plum blossoms
bestowed by wind and neglect
then discovered like a shuffled card
from a deck of tricks,
leaving you in awe of all that is offered.

GIFTING MY MARACUYÁ

A stringy vine that gets tangled
in shoes laces, or around bare ankles,
it's best to let it creep
up tall trees in broad sun,
no shade to hide its bloom,
but I have shade and stumbles,
so I gave my Maracuyá vines away
to settle in a sunnier clime.
Years passed and the vine flowered
a ripe passionate purple mass
of petals and filament and corona.
We forget all we give away
until it returns fully ripened.
A stringy vine in another's soil,
blossoming flower into fruit and passion,
returned as a gift bestowed
by giving love away.

My Son's Sweatshirt

Father and son come by,
tell me they are going camping
into woods, bear country, past scorpion rock
to black lakes carpeted with lichen stones visible
only by toe-touch.

I worry about my son's pearl tipped toes
scraping all things jagged in dark pools having no
bottom.

I tell him what to pack for this time with his father,
remind my son that he was named for survival,
I open the drawer where he keeps his warm clothes.

After they leave, and the car disappears
into a single lane curve leading to thinner air,
when I can no longer see the trail of exhaust,
I turn back into the house
and see my son's sweatshirt—forgotten.

Its rumpled form, deserted by the body of my son,
this gift I continuously give to his father—
a father who I hope remembers
that in the woods, there are no sonatas to perfect,
and long division is just a maze of Manzanita bush.

I hang up the sweatshirt,
its collar pinned to a hook,
tonight my son will know the cold

and the sound of high mountain wind,
the only whisper tucking him in.

WISHES FOR ENGLISH 101 STUDENTS
After Lucille Clifton's poem, *"Wishes For Sons"*

I wish them blank stares, thirty-five at a time,
I wish them the shuffle of bored feet,
fragments, run-ons, and the inconsistencies
of verbs looking for agreement.

I wish them doodles and dropped eyelids,
then the dream of standing naked
in a filled to capacity auditorium,
their lecture notes containing the wisdom of a fig
leaf.

I wish them red-ink stains on fingertips,
folders of ungraded papers on Friday night,
later, lost folders of graded papers on Monday
morning.

And when they deem themselves ready to graduate,
I wish them the course that they forgot to take.

FLASH FLOOD

Between the Picasso and the pans,
warm clothes or love letters written
when weather did not point its threatened finger,
what would I take?

All that can be carried by hand,
or kept in a jean pocket.
In various keys your harmonicas
strewn on the dresser are in perfect pitch.
In disasters of heart,
is there such a thing as basic survival?

In this flash flood of fury,
I hear the bending notes of the harp
what is it that we really need—

warmth, bread, water
your shrilling high C,
the high seas of my anger—
a blues riff,

or the breaking waves of music?

PORTULACA IN SHADOW
for Michelle

August in L.A.,

a litany of the familiar—
delphinium, dianthus, columbine—
each flower a vise on the redolent pocket of time.

You seek deliverance
among red palmed petals of portulaca,
transplanted from a garden in Vietnam,
now wrapped tight in evening's bud.

What grows in L.A.

is common to both lands,
and you listen for sounds of Asian gardens—
bamboo creaking in an October wind,

bike wheels on gravel,
the clink of a teaspoon
against the cobalt rim of china
and in high grass, feline declarations.

But, here, in L.A.

under the drone of imminent freeways,
the purple vine of morning glory
chokes the trellis and the memory

of an egret's call ascending
from rice fields pales
against the clamor of the angel's city.

An unspeakable loneliness
claims your life as the past
clenches shut, like portulaca in shadow.

STEVEN, STEVEN

To each other we'd taunt:
What are you gonna do when I'm gone?
Think of distant lands, forbidden romance,
and none of the tedium of who left the kitchen
light on.

Then, there came the night you were dying—
splayed across black and white
checkered tiles on the bathroom floor.

I can not fathom what I felt then,
only the image of your fading eyes
rolled back in your head,
far away from me.

But you came back, asked:
did I worry not knowing the password
to the latest bank account,
or the location of the key
to the safety deposit box?

I did not think about that, not at all.
I do not know what I thought then,
I only remember screaming your name,
I can only remember screaming your name.

THE GINGER JAR

I wore your shirt for days
after you left,
lingered in the smell of one
who moved in checked patterns.

When hurt, I clean,
crumbs coaxed from the underbelly
of webs curtained with hair and dander.
Matted strands of broom
whisk away the disorder of crevices.

I dust the Chinese ginger jar
your gift to mark an eve or year,
our time lost in all that's familiar,
no longer belonging to us.

I want to dust your gift clean,
center it on memory's shelf
but when I take hold
the jar slips from my hands,

our seasons shatter, mar the porcelain shine,
cobalt dragons and butterflies,
the past's unerring score
stored inside its ivory finish, splatter

over the shine of newly waxed linoleum.

"I sense the spreading of a wing."

Osip Mandelstam

7 WAYS TO LOOK AT LONELINESS

While most are tangled in dreams,
I move in star strained darkness,
wrestling sorrow.

I pass closed doors to rooms,
where people I love,
no longer sleep.

From empty spaces
I think a voice comes,
but it is just rattling panes,

or a spoon clanking
against a china cup:
Tea for one.

The clenched fist
of clouds open
on evening's reign.

Heir to dreams
so many covers
blanket the bed.

A slivered wind
chills the empty side
waiting for your return,

                              or the waxing moon.

WHAT CATCHES DREAMS

My son and I traveled long,
a continent between us,
to visit the dying.
When the air in the house
started to reek of stale sputum and loss,
we left for a walk.

In a dollar store
we found dream catchers
with beads the color of blood
and feathers limp in the stagnant Florida breeze.

The reduced price tag read:

> *"A gift of protection:*
> *good dreams will be remembered,*
> *and bad entangled in the web."*

I bought and believed,
though moments away, in a silent house,
a grandfather lay—void of dreams,
or the shield of bead and feather,
his waxing sorrows entangled
in the web and marrow of regret.

Far now from Florida and a funeral behind,
spent reveries splash on winter mornings,
worn feathered streamers dangle above my waking.

Each day begins with a belief in beaded myths,

and wishes for my son, in distant places,
rising into his own dreams, so remote from mine,
protected only by a sinewy web.

SAKURA

My father is dying,
this news, in late April,
reaches us in northern Japan, and we argue
about how to feel.

Outside, *sakura*, cherry blossoms, are blooming.

Spring's axiom can not bail our moods,
and when angry, you clean, like a woman
burrowed in drawers, dark, dank arenas,
a search for the unneeded.

On the kitchen table, a pile of uncertainties,
among broken staplers, hair clips
and mismatched earrings, my old poems,
words locking us to decades,

and I do not know — which to toss, what to keep?

April's seasonal Honshu wind rips
the remaining *sakura* onto pavements pale,
flurries of blanched pink blossoms
now a ground cover.

Across an ocean,
my father is on dialysis,
my mother calls, says
"He can survive like this."

Sick and senile, my father's days
are like discarded words,
those we toss, those we keep,
those we hope for.

OVER FIFTY

We're likened to flowers—
delphinium, crocus, forsythia—
names that color the raspy throat of time,
fill the air with familiar gray tones,

but consider the hydrangea,
kindred to diminished hues of November
it shutters from wine to teal till petals
gleam like burnt sapphires, pearls, bronze.

Pansies, petunias, zinnias
in their crimson dresses
tear in October's rush of wind,

the hydrangea remains steadfast
bleached from wind and time its colors turn
from lavender to sea-shades,

turn from summer's incense
to the perch of night with distant
sounds of bells and strength of chimes.

VISIBLE

Cat calls,
now are real screeches
I hear, at midnight, from my bed facing an alley.

No one wants to help me change a tire.

The black, low cut dress does not work, nor even
fit

yet, I dance
with feet alight,
no one watches.

In torn, stained tees, I walk without fear

of anyone following, or calling, or grabbing
I can curse aloud,
no one hears, when I say:

I am here,
I have proof,
lines, scars, the stretchy skin

I still live in.

If I Had a Cat's 9 Lives

I would live the first three to hide
under the bed, in the laundry room,
or under the Volvo parked
in an unpaved driveway.

When it came time for me to shed that
scary cat skin, only because someone kind fed me,
I would venture across lawns to hunt.

Perhaps the next few lives would be lived
close to where I hid, but a tad more in the open
letting strangers extend a tentative hand
for me to brush against.
Then perhaps, I would let them scratch my nose.

In my fifth life,
I would take to the alleys
and mark my territory,
allowing no one in,
and sharpen my claws
against the tired oaks.

Then skinny, hungry, and winter weary,
I may purr those lingering last lives
in a home where children pull at my mangey tail
while I am skittish on catnip.

But, that ninth life,
I am saving for you,
who have crossed borders,

witnessed well, lived fruitfully,
and know the importance
of a warm and welcoming lap.

PALIMPSEST

Our bodies,
a palimpsest of sorts,
each new touch, an etching
on the terrace
of scrubbed memories.

Your hand upon my skin,
a caress more than the layering
of body upon body,
of heat upon heat.

What we seek in touch
robs us of words,
every caress bears a trace
of our coupled history
bearing the scars
that scratch the canvas.

FINDING THE TRIBE

On days when the air is rife
with scent and breeze
and there is no anger
toward any living thing,
on those days help the bone thin
lift packages from step to door frame,
hold open that same heavy glass door,
so the mother of three can balance
carriage and carry.
There comes a day,
when a neighbor needs to know
how to use something other than the landline
in order to see a grandchild in a state
with different borders.
Summer days, bring a box of donuts
to someone stuck at a desk,
and pick a bouquet of wild asters,
so affordable, pick bunches
for tables where all are invited to sit,
for it is in the invites that we find a tribe,
and relearn how to help, to praise, to share,
and how to come home.

WHY I DID NOT GO TO YOUR POETRY READING

Four days now that he's been asking me to help
till the soil so we can plant wildflowers
over that grayish patch of decomposing weeds.

The same time as your poetry reading
that I wanted to attend, but didn't—
I was helping my husband plant wildflowers,
with names like alyssum, delphinium, and
zinnia—
names you would have in your poems.

You're a good poet.
You share everyday epiphanies.
Yes, poetry saves us,
and I hate to not attend,
but it's not like I'm missing
my son's 2nd grade piano recital,
or chickening out at the blood drive
for earthquake victims.

You are just another poet.
Inspiring, spouting wisdom and truth,
but won't those wildflowers do the same thing?
One is silver and the other gold.

PINKY PROMISE

It is the first promise
one swears to—

tiny fingers entwined
hooked and anchored
a world contained in a promise,
tight as silken thread in the eye of a needle.

In the landscape of oaths,
there is power in the pinky latched,
the fist unfurling, the silken thread
stitching an unspoken vow—
    Let us be lovers,

and trust in an unmoored anchor,
a waxing pearl moon, and a constant star,
guides on a timeless journey.

WHAT WE WAIT FOR

The black whiskered vireo
landed on the wood-planked railing,
seeing only what was directly ahead.

We waited and watched, yielding,
not to threaten or disturb a simple presence
held only for what lies in the sphere of sight,
on wood, on railing, on bridge, or under sky.

It is all about patience and who relents,
who walks on, who whispers first,
relinquishing wonder, treading ahead,
past the sound of fluttering wings.

WINTER IS ON ITS WAY

A tundra of cold settles into the heart,
and we know that winter will walk
into the rest of our lives,
and cold, like glass, can shatter and spread
into the tiniest dusty covered corners.
But the train of winter's fury also slows and readies
to pull into a station where people disembark
onto a platform of noise and color and shops
that sell warm things like hats and cappuccinos,
and the heart is heard, not silenced
in white space or a snowy blur,
but ready for the thaw.

THE KNOCKING

You are inside now,
a blizzard of loneliness
whispers through the keyhole.
Sadness locks in like the sleeping
cat on a windowsill.
You can't remember where you were
When that door slammed
the heart out of you.
Inside and out,
it is the same cold front,
the door cannot close against—
but there comes a knocking,
there always comes a knocking,
that is why we have doors: inside, out, slam
There comes a knocking—

Open up.

THE BEST LAID PLANS

An injured bird in the driveway
that is what went awry on the morning
we were about to celebrate
the day that we met, 53 years ago,
in front of a now demolished bar in Brooklyn.

Our aging plans, breakfast, and a walk,
deterred when we scooped the mourning dove,
named for peaceful memories,
into an old shoebox and drove
45 minutes to a sanctuary ensuring its rescue.

The bird fell out of a nest,
injured a wing, and weeks later,
when I tracked its recovery,
the message said *Your bird is thriving.*

Don't we all have injured wings,
yet manage to survive
the random rescues of heart,
and in our best laid plans, we thrive.

R.I.P.

Why waste space and soil?
I want to be cremated,
so few visit me in living,
who will visit in death?

I would rather weeds crawl
on stone than words in an epitaph,
but if I had a gravesite,
I would want it to say:
Rest in Poetry.

For only in poetry is there rest
from madness, which is funneled
into tight stanzas that often compare
lives to flowers, for flowers against stone
seem to thrive on a hard, rough surface
and are never angry.

AKNOWLEDGMENTS

This poet is grateful to the following magazines for publishing the listed poems:

One Art: "Anniversary, Again" Nominated for a Pushcart Prize, 2022, "My Son's Sweatshirt"

Awakenings: "A Howl in the Wind: A Response to the Overturning of Roe v. Wade" Nominated for a Pushcart Prize 2022

Gyroscope Review: "Old Couple Cutting Watermelon"

Eunoia Review: "Flash Flood," "Sakura"

Red Eft Review: "Twigs and Trinkets"

Rat's Ass Review: "What the Dead Can Use"

Amethyst Review: "Gifting My Maracuyá"

Last Leaves: "Finding the Tribe"

Oye Drum: "Balance,"

Masticadores: "Prayer", "My Wisteria", "First Banana", "The Empty Heart", "7 Ways to Look at Loneliness"

Synchronized Chaos: "North of Sorrow" "Palimpsest"

Beatnik Cowboy: "If I Had a Cat's Nine Lives"

Up Your Ars Poetry Anthology: "Why I Did Not Go To Your Poetry Reading"

THANKS:

Heaps of gratitude to Constance Brewer, editor of Gyroscope Press for keen and generous editing.

Hugs (in no specific order) to my daily muses, Robyne, Ruby, Maggie, Carol, Joix, Katie, Dr. Carol, Michelle, Irene, Judy, Corey, Margo, Nancy, T.R., Susan, Jenny, Margaret, Pam, Paula, Suzanne, Teresa, Epstein, A.L., Laura, Lucia, and Alison, so many sisters.

And, to my forever muse, Steven, so many poems.

ABOUT THE AUTHOR

Laurie Kuntz is an award-winning poet and film producer. She taught creative writing and poetry in Japan, Thailand and the Philippines. Many of her poetic themes are a result of her working with Southeast Asian refugees in refugee camps in Thailand and the Philippines for over a decade after the Vietnam War years. She holds an MFA in Writing from Vermont College.

She has published six poetry collections (*That Infinite Roar*, Gyroscope Press, *Talking Me Off The Roof*, Kelsay Books, The *Moon Over My Mother's House*, Finishing Line Press, *Simple Gestures*, Texas Review Press, *Women at the Onsen*, Blue Light Press and *Somewhere in the Telling*, Mellen Press). *Simple Gestures*, won the Texas Review Poetry Chapbook Contest, and *Women at the Onsen* won the Blue Light Press Chapbook Contest. She has been nominated for three Pushcart Prizes and two Best of the Net Prizes.

Her work has been published in *Gyroscope Review, Roanoke Review, Third Wednesday, One Art, Sheila Na Gig, The Bloomsbury Review, The MacGuffin, The Louisville Review, The Charlotte Poetry Review, The Roanoke Review, The Southern Review, The New Virginia Review, The South Florida Review,* and many other literary journals and anthologies.

She produced the documentaries, *Do Tell*, on the repeal of the Don't Ask, Don't Tell Law, and *Strangers to Peace*, a documentary on the Colombian peace process and reintegration of guerrilla soldiers in Colombia.
Visit her at:
https://lauriekuntz.myportfolio.com/home-1

Gyroscope Press
Constance Brewer, Publisher
PO Box 1989
Gillette, WY 82718
gyroscopepress@gmail.com

Made in the USA
Columbia, SC
20 November 2023

26565096R00038